TAROT of the KINGDOMS

Paige Ozma Ashmore

REDFeather™

MIND | BODY | SPIRIT

4880 Lower Valley Road, Atglen, PA 19310

Library of Congress Control Number: 2019947648

Designed by Danielle D. Farmer
Cover design by Danielle D. Farmer
Card illustrations by: Paige Ashmore

Type set in Poor Richard/Mightype Script/Aileron

ISBN: 978-0-7643-5963-7
Printed in China

Published by Red Feather Mind, Body, Spirit
An imprint of Schiffer Publishing, Ltd.
4880 Lower Valley Road
Atglen, PA 19310
Phone: (610) 593-1777; Fax: (610) 593-2002
E-mail: info@schifferbooks.com
Web: www.redfeathermbs.com

Acknowledgments

I would like to thank Pete Schiffer for agreeing to publish this project and Carey Massimini for helping with my questions at the very beginning. I would like to thank my editor, Dinah Roseberry, and designer, Danielle Farmer, for their wisdom and suggestions in making this project the best it could ever be. It has proven invaluable to me. I would also like to thank Mary Versosky, who has been with me since the beginning, when it was just an idea. I am grateful for Carol Japngie Horton and Faith Rayne for their being there for me in many ways as well. May you all be blessed beyond imagining!

Contents

The Invitation

This deck is an invitation from the magical world to you, dear reader. The realms of tree spirits, fairies, merfolk, angels, and dragons want you to remember that once you had your own kingdom next to theirs. You even have your own card in this deck called Spirit to commemorate that! How lovely!

They invite you at this time in the planet's history, to join hands again, and dance with them. Don't worry about the choreography; there isn't any. A spontaneous dance of the heart invents its own steps as you are inspired. The time is now for furious dancing, for remembering, for reclaiming.

Introduction

Tarot of the Kingdoms came about like this: For many years, I have been approached to create a Tarot deck. As both an artist and a Tarot reader for thirty years, I found the idea intriguing. But what could I create that would stand alone and be unique? There had been so much said about Tarot already.

At that point, I received a gentle tap on the shoulder that felt like the tingling brush of a fairy's wing. I listened.

The very invitation that has been extended to you was then given to me. I am happy to say I accepted, and because of the dancing and long, magical conversations between myself and the denizens of these magical worlds, you now have this deck in your hands.

Anyone can learn how to listen to the secret world. I am speaking of the four directions: north, east, south, and west. Respectively in these worlds live the fairies (East); the dragons, angels, and a lovely phoenix (South); the merfolk (West); and the tree spirits (North). These are the four kingdoms. The fifth kingdom, Spirit, is the place where we live as one.

Spirit permeates all things. Those from the other realms want us to know that there is a part of us that is of them, so we live in each of those kingdoms. Together, we are the Five Kingdoms, and the fifth element is love—our true nature.

This deck will provide direction because it is a deck of the compass points of spirit.

Chapter One
Let's Go to the Movies

WHEN I teach people how to read cards, I like to use a technique that takes only five minutes, and I've taught many people to read brilliantly with this method.

> Take any Tarot deck and shuffle it. Fan it out face down. Now think of a question. Let the question go.

Pretend you are going to the movies. You don't know what's out there to see. You've just decided you're going to go and pick your movie based on the movie poster. With popcorn in hand, choose one card and flip it over. This is your movie.

Don't worry about what the writing on the card says. Just go into the picture.

> What kind of movie is this? What do you think will happen in it? How will it end?

Play with this method. When you think of your card as a movie, it can open creative doors of exploration, and new ideas emerge from this. It also builds trust in your unique way of visioning things.

Chapter Two
The Deck Full of Stories

A STANDARD Tarot deck contains the Minor Arcana, which consist of four suits, and the Major Arcana, which are the 22 trumps.

Unlike other Tarot decks, there is a fifth suit with one card only in *Tarot of the Kingdoms*. This suit, Spirit, represents the Oneness that permeates all things. When the cards are read, you can use this card as the querent (the person for whom the reading is done) or see where it falls in a reading by shuffling it with the rest of the deck. If you are reading for yourself, Spirit represents you. If you are reading for someone else, Spirit represents them.

The suits in the Minor Arcana, other than Spirit are the following:

The Suit of Air, hailing from the direction of the East on the compass of Soul, equates to the Wands suit in the Rider Waite system. The beings that herald from the East, home of air magic, are the fairies. The fairies know how the air sparkles. When you quiet the mind and sit in the presence of a flower, you can see or feel the air sparkling with potential. You can activate this kind of magic by asking the question "What wants to be created next?"

The Suit of Fire, hailing from the direction of the South on the compass of Soul, equates to the suit of Swords in the Rider Waite system. The beings that herald from the South, home of fire magic, are the dragons, the angels, and a phoenix. These beings are all about passion, particularly the dragons. The angels represent how that passion can be best channeled, and the phoenix will rise from the ashes of cosmic change.

The Suit of Water, hailing from the direction of the West on the compass of Soul, equates to the Cups suit in the Rider Waite system. The beings of the West are the merfolk who live in the place of dreaming magic, of memories, of love and the emotions. Your emotions are what you use as fuel to make magic happen in your life. They show you how to do this.

The Suit of Earth, hailing from the direction of the North on the compass of Soul, equates to the pentacles suit in the Rider Waite system. The beings depicted here are Tree Spirits. Trees understand gratitude. Your health and wealth in life are all balanced around your ability to give and receive. Trees give us oxygen, and we give them carbon dioxide. We support each other.

The Major Arcana consists of 22 cards. These cards have their own personality and represent ancient forces that are at work in the universe, particularly in the form of archetypes. An archetype is a symbol that is commonly shared among people of different cultures. These archetypes revealed themselves as ancient, sentient beings that exist in the Unseen World and are full of stories based on what they represent. Each card has its own story and guidance to offer you.

The Universe card is a stand-alone card, belonging to neither the Major nor Minor Arcana. When it appears in a reading, there is an invitation to see things from a larger perspective. It might suggest that the querent is being either too small minded or small actioned about something. It's an invitation to sit with the part of you that is you as Divine.

After each description of a card is the "Divinatory Meaning," which foretells the magic of the card and the "Direction to Take," which is guidance on how you can use that magic.

Chapter Three
Layouts

BELOW are three different layouts. I believe in keeping things simple, and so do the kingdoms. You can use other layouts of your choice that are not described here, of course. These are here as alternatives.

ONE-CARD LAYOUT

Shuffle the cards while dwelling on a question, then randomly pull one card. This card can be seen as an overall theme to your question. It can suggest guidance or what you most need to know about your question.

THREE-CARD LAYOUT

Shuffle the cards. When ready, lay one card for position one. This represents the present. To the left of position one place card number two. This represents the past. To the right of position one, place card number three. This represents the future.

If you choose, you can pull an extra card and, before doing so, connect with the kingdoms and ask, "What do I most need to know to activate the highest light in this situation?" Then pull a fourth clarifier card. You can also do this with the other spreads.

PAST   PRESENT   FUTURE

PENTACLE SPREAD

This spread covers all the areas of life most people have. The five positions are for Spirit (representing the final outcome), Fire (representing what you're dwelling on in regard to the question in mind), Air (the energy for change around the question), Water (other people in your life, particularly family and friends, significant others), and Earth (usually your job, your health, and money in your life). The positions form the five points on a pentacle.

1.   Spirit is laid down first and is the top point of the pentacle.
2.   Fire is laid down second and is the lower right point of the pentacle.
3.   Air is laid down third and is the upper left point of the pentacle.
4.   Water is laid down fourth and is the upper right point of the pentacle.
5.   Earth is laid down last and is the lower left point of the pentacle.

Intriguingly, the final outcome is laid out first. This expresses the spiritual concept that all things are created first in the realm of Spirit before they are made manifest. It acknowledges us as creator beings.

13

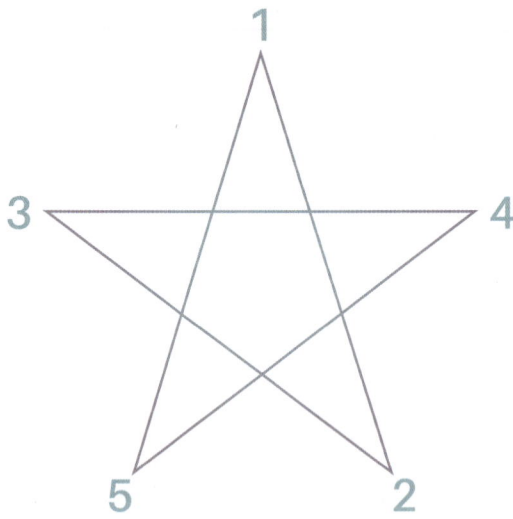

The reading addresses how all areas of your life are affected by the question. Particularly, pay attention to the Fire position. This placement can talk about what the querent is really thinking about concerning their question.

Chapter Four

Tarot and Numerology

A VERY simple way of learning Tarot is by understanding numerology. Numerology acts like a Rosetta stone that can unlock the meanings of the cards once you understand it. Think of the number of the card as a theme, if you will.

One: Aces equate to the number one and talk about beginnings. Hence, all the aces in the suits of Tarot would equate to some form of beginning. Nothing is formed yet, but there is an initial "Aha!" moment. There is the birth of a new idea taking shape.

Two: Twos build on the aces. Here, energy begins to swirl around the idea begun in the ace, and it begins to move, seeking form. Twos also indicate partnerships, either the meeting of new people or the desire to partner. Our dear ace wants to collaborate so it can have form and become physically manifest, but it hasn't yet. Planning often happens here.

Three: Manifestation into physical form happens with the three. Threes are where the idea of the ace, having found reciprocity in the universe through the two, is now made

manifest. When two people come together and have a child, that is the energy of the three happening. As an aside, the heart has three numbers associated with it, and they are the numbers three, six, and nine. Three symbolizes self love, as well as romantic love.

Four: Fours build stability. Now that your project has physical form in the three, it needs to stabilize. A table has four legs; an automobile has four tires. Fours are where you get your land legs under you. A lot of the time, the four energy can talk about holding space for where you're at in the moment. Once something has been created, you take a breath and lock it in, so to speak. You do something to anchor that energy of manifestation, which can come through gratitude or meditating—both excellent exercises in getting your manifestation to stick.

Five: The reason you want to stabilize is because afterward, you hit the energy of the fives. Fives traditionally represent karma in Tarot. After your creation has stabilized, the universe will show up and shake your table to make sure it's solid. Does it stand? Or is the foundation not so solid, and it falls? Here's the secret about fives: They are also numbers of abundance and prosperity. When you get shaken up in life, it can help you course correct and put you on the path that is really going to blow it open for you in a positive way. When fives show up in a reading, look for that hidden pot of gold.

Six: Following the shake-up of the fives, we encounter the assistance found in the six energy. What happens when life shakes you up? You ask for help and the universe

supplies it. Sixes hold the energy of help and assistance. They are the second of the three heart numbers. Whereas the three represents love found in the coupling of the two energy, sixes represent the love found in the family or your community.

Seven: Sevens are numbers of introspection. Deeply intuitive in nature, they can be isolating because that inner journey can go deep into the self. Seven is a number of intuition. Sometimes when you can see truth clearly, it can cause you to not trust other people or situations in life, so sevens can represent feeling like you're at a crossroads where you're trying to figure out what's true for you. After the chaos of the five energy and receiving assistance in the six, it's natural to question things and think about where you might have been off in the past.

Eight: Eights talk about learning and are ready to put the deep thought in the seven and the gratitude from the six for the assistance into the furthering of the dream. There is work happening here, and realigning with abundance. You're willing to learn something new, work diligently, and go exploring for what is truly right for you and your purpose.

Nine: Nines are the third number in the heart series. Here, the nine represents love of all: of humanity, of creation, of our link with all the beings of the directions. Nines reexamine the realm of what's real and what isn't. Where is your truth? A nine can either fulfill you or make you go deeper into questioning what your reality is and what's right for you.

Ten: Tens are the ultimate goal and apex of what a suit wants to express itself as. It represents the completion and pinnacle of your idea, project, or goal. In this deck, it bears the ultimate message the beings of a particular suit want you to know. Completion.

If there is a predominance of any number in a reading, pay attention to the message for that particular number. Following is a list.

A predominance of

Ones: This is a time for planning new things and taking that first step.

Twos: Start connecting with others on your creations, move the energy, collaborate.

Threes: Manifesting is occurring in your life. Build it. As one of the three heart numbers, it can also represent an emphasis on significant personal relationships in your life and can suggest deepening the one with yourself.

Fours: Take a breath. Check in with yourself. Where can you hold space and experience gratitude? Meditate.

Fives: Where is your source for stability? Look for that, because that's where your gold is.

Sixes: Don't be afraid to ask for help—or give it. As one of the three heart numbers, it's about connecting more with what family is for you.

Sevens: Reflect, go inside. Trust your intuition.

Eights: Work it. Be willing to learn something more about what you're already engaged in.

Nines: Look deeper. There is some new information that wants to emerge. As one of the three heart numbers, it talks about connecting with a larger community and perhaps the need for that.

Tens: Projects are completing. Things are reaching their apex. What's next?

The Suite of
Archetypes

0 The Fool

The Archetype of The Fool wanted to wear the costume of a lone bear cub who has grown past the point of living with her mother. In the world of bears, mother bears are fierce protectors of their cubs until they reach the age of two years, and then they are driven away to survive on their own.

If you look at the pattern of the stars above her head, you will see the constellation of the Great Bear. This bear cub is made of the stuff of stars and is part of the Divine Universe. She is always watched over and guided by the greatest of bears, the Celestial Bear, even though she can't see it.

That's the nature of The Fool card—aligning with your Truth and trusting in what you can't see. But you can feel it.

Divinatory Meaning:
A new journey where you must trust the truth within. A brand-new slate.

Direction to Take:
Trust in what you cannot see.

O The Fool

1 The Magician

What is being depicted in the card of The Magician is a deer dancer. She dances between the worlds. Part human and part deer, she represents the true essence of magic. Once you encounter the lessons of The Fool and you learn to trust your own inner voice, you can come to a place where your magic is.

Divinatory Meaning:
You already have everything you need to create something that is good and beautiful in your life. Manifestation.

Direction to Take:
Start that project, build that dream. Take the first step.

I The Magician

2 The High Priestess

Sitting on a lotus that rises from the primordial sea, The High Priestess, as a fox goddess, holds a symbol of life, a simple leaf. She is deeply connected with her wild nature, and her gown is the sea that supports all life. She sits between two pillars that represent duality—the world of day and the secrets of night. Behind her is the pink dawning sky, where the two times of day meet. She has learned to embrace the Divine Fool, dance her power with The Magician, and now, because of this, has arrived at a deeper mystery.

Divinatory Meaning:
Protect your magic. You know the answers right now but don't have to spill the beans about it right now.

Direction to Take:
You know what's really going on, but keep your own counsel. Also, sometimes when The High Priestess shows up in a reading, it means part of what you are asking about will remain a mystery. The Universe may not be willing to tell you everything yet. There's usually a good reason why. Trust that it has your back.

2 The High Priestess

3 The Empress

Look at this abundant Earth Goddess! All the wealth of the world blooms on her corpulent, curvy body. She is even crowned in the golden glory of autumn, that season of delicious, warm soups and savory breads for dipping. When was the last time you really enjoyed the taste of food? Or the touch of a lover? Or held your own beautiful body in your own arms? This beautiful goddess, with her eyes lightly closed, is dreaming dreams of abundance, wealth, prosperity, and creativity. She is life longing for itself.

Divinatory Meaning:
Wealth, abundance, creativity. Life is juicy.

Direction to Take:
Spend time creating something. Make art, plant a garden, build a business, bake cookies, or let yourself fall in love with life.

3 The Empress

4 The Emperor

If you know your horses, then you know it's the lead mare that leads a herd of horses. The same is true of elephants and reindeer—both are led by the lead matriarch. In a herd of horses, the lead mare is the one dominant female who knows herself, being deeply connected with her instinct. She leads her herd to water and is the first to drink. She leads her herd to grazing pastures and is the first to eat. The job of the protector goes to the stallion. His job is to enforce the will of the lead mare. The stallion keeps the herd safe by safeguarding her will.

The Empress creates, and The Emperor ensures that her creation is protected, and enforces boundaries as set by her so that can happen.

Divinatory Meaning:

Honor your boundaries. If not well aspected by other cards around it, this card can sometimes indicate a controlling, manipulative person in your life, because these people don't value boundaries.

Direction to Take:

You need to be more assertive about something in your life. Also, it can be time to put your spiritual plans into action. Set boundaries with someone.

4 The Emperor

5 The Hierophant

There is an ancient Chinese legend that tells the story of a cosmic sea turtle who lives at the bottom of the ocean, and every 100,000 years it surfaces and searches the world for all of the best wisdom, knowledge, and creativity that has existed during that time. When the Cosmic Sea Turtle finds this knowledge, she gathers it into her body, which doubles as a great library, and descends back into the depths of the sea.

On the bottom of the image of this turtle is the pattern of the Kabbalistic Tree of Life, further uniting it with the idea of great wisdom and knowledge.

Divinatory Meaning:
Working with an establishment that has a long history attached to it. Receiving a blessing. Higher education.

Direction to Take:
There is something deeper calling to you. Go exploring for what is seeking you, whether that indicates you explore your local bookstore, go back to school, or travel to search for what is speaking to you on a level of soul. If you're looking for a job, this is about doing a regular nine-to-five gig over anything entrepreneurial.

33

6 The Lovers

Love has a liminal quality about it.

When you think about it, humans live in the liminal world. The sky isn't just something that floats high over the Earth—it touches the Earth. Only the very bottoms of our feet actually touch the Earth, so when you think about it, we are always walking in the sky.

Love—true love—exists in the liminal world because it's where two people touch each other, while still retaining their uniqueness and their sovereignty. The sun loves the Earth. He illuminates her during the day, and rainbows happen when the sun sends the Earth love letters.

Divinatory Meaning:
Love entering your life. This card can also represent choosing between two things.

Direction to Take:
This card can appear when you have multiple options facing you, and you don't know which direction to take. Think about a yes or no question regarding your situation. Close your eyes and take three, full, deep breaths. Open your eyes and look at this card. Do you first see the night at the bottom of the card or the daylight at the top of the card? Night means no or wait. The time isn't right yet. Day means yes.

6 The Lovers

7 The Chariot

The great panda symbolizes the unity of yin and yang, dark and light, positivity and negativity. Astride the panda is an alchemist who can make music that summons spring, which bursts forth in riotous bloom from the playing of her golden flute. Allow the gentle sense of natural direction the panda embodies to be your Chariot.

Divinatory Meaning:
Moving forward in life in a powerful way. Self-mastery. Sometimes indicates an actual move or a long-distance trip.

Direction to Take:
Go on a journey. Especially if you're confused, taking a small trip or traveling somewhere can give you fresh perspective.

7 The Chariot

8 Strength

The Strength card depicts a Mayan huntress who is blending with a jaguar that walks beside her, becoming one with her strength. This piece is based on a legend around the Mayan people. There was a mass, unexplained disappearance of the Mayan people around the time of the arrival of the Spanish conquistadors during their discovery of the New World. What really happened was that the Mayan people realized they didn't want to be suppressed under Spanish rule, so the majority of them got together, turned into jaguars, and went to live in the surrounding rainforest. It is said that if you sit at the base of the rainforest and be patient, the jaguars will come down from the trees, turn back into people, and tell you their stories.

Divinatory Meaning:
Stand in your power. Remember that you're wearing a crown, and embrace the quality of royalty. Patience.

Direction to Take:
The step here is all about perseverance and learning how to wait for things. But it's also about valuing yourself. When you get up in the morning, stand before your mirror, close your eyes, and pretend you are wearing a crown. Feel the weight of it. Now carry yourself throughout the day as a royal.

8 Strength

9 The Hermit

The Hermit in this card is portrayed by a Dervish—a Sufi Mystic. He lives in the desert alone and holds the flowering branch of life. He is always laughing because he has discovered the great cosmic truth of life. Ever joyful, he realizes that he is the Source of his own light.

Divinatory Meaning:
Spend some time alone. A solitary period in life. Also it can indicate finding or becoming a teacher.

Direction to Take:
A lot of people fight those periods of isolation that turn up. You'll want to talk to people, but you get the answering machine when you call, and whatever it is you want to talk about seems critical. When this happens, it means you have your own answers, and you hate hearing that, but when you relax into it, you can find your own truth.

9 The Hermit

10 The Wheel of Fortune

The Wheel of Fortune talks about the karmic pattern of how things happen in life. In this image the tiger has brought down the deer, and part of the body of the tiger forms the grass the deer is eating. The truth is that the tiger will die one day and become part of the Earth, nourishing the soil with the nutrients from her body. Then the grass will grow and the deer will eat that grass that was once a tiger.

Divinatory Meaning:
Major life changes are afoot.

Direction to Take:
Breathe.

10 The Wheel of Fortune

11 Justice

The shaman at the bottom of this picture holds a wand, which she uses to invoke the path symbolized by the spiral leading to the heart above her. A red wolf sits on top of the spiral and is who the priestess is in the depths of her wild heart. The hands of humanity in the roots of the tree represent her spiritual ancestry. The Justice card embodies choice, because justice will choose one side over another. This Justice card invites you to explore the path that honors you and your authenticity through choice.

Divinatory Meaning:

There's a rightness to life happening right now. Things will work out fairly for you. Great card for victory in legal matters. This is also a card about stepping up to your life in a powerful way.

Direction to Take:

It's time to make a decision about something in your life. Like the red-wolf shaman, seize the day and choose your direction.

11 Justice

12 The Hanged Man

This whale is beautifully supported by the ocean, and even though this creature weighs several tons, it is as light as a feather floating in all of that blue water. How can you let yourself be lifted by the Universe today? Whale is asking you this. Whale is here because the Hanged Man is traditionally a card of sacrifice and seeing things from a new perspective. Because Whale makes its home in the seas—the amniotic fluid of Mother Earth—Whale hears all perspectives by listening to the world's stories.

Divinatory Meaning:

Seeing things from a new perspective. This is also another card that can talk about a suspended period of waiting in your life where patience is needed. Sometimes you have to sacrifice something to achieve your goals, and that could be your point of view on something.

Direction to Take:

Go outside during the sunrise or sunset and look at the horizon. Now turn to the side and bend at the hips so that your body forms a 90-degree angle. Look at the sunset from this position. From this perspective, you can see the curvature of the Earth and get the feeling that the Earth is revolving. It can open a sense of awe in you if you let it, and just this simple exercise can open a startling new perspective on things in your life.

12 The Hanged Man

13 Death

According to the most ancient telling, Persephone was out gathering flowers with her mother, Demeter, the Earth Goddess. Persephone heard the cries of the dead, and when she followed the sound of their mourning, she discovered that they couldn't find their way to the Underworld. She told them she knew the way and led them down into the depths. Once there, she realized that she didn't understand the mysteries of death, only knowing about blooming and life. Hades, the Lord of the Underworld, said he would teach her, and in the process of that learning, she fell in love with him. Here she is, leading the souls, which show up as orbs, to the Underworld.

Divinatory Meaning:
A change in your life brings your old life to an end. New things beckon.

Direction to Take:
There is an invitation for change appearing in your life. The direction to take when considering this is to boldly be present and look around for what hasn't been working. Don't feed the fears around it; move forward.

13 Death

14 Temperance

The Angel of Temperance is a goddess whose body is made from the four elements. Spirit, the fifth element, is present in who she is as a being of power. Wild birds attend her.

Divinatory Meaning:
Wait for it. It will come to you, because that which you are seeking is also seeking you. A time of integration and healing is approaching.

Direction to Take:
Balance between work and play. Where can you bring some moderation into your life?

14 Temperance

15 The Devil

You've been invited for tea! How grand! And who's that waiting for you with a cup of tea in her hands? Why it's Grandmother Coyote! Oy, you're in for a treat!

Yep, that empty seat is for you, my dear! Excited? You should be, or maybe you should be shaking in your boots, but it's all good. She is the wise grandmother in trickster form. The truth is that Grandmother Coyote adores you, but sometimes she needs to trick you into seeing your fortune.

Divinatory Meaning:
This is about being stuck in a rut—feeling that you need to change, but not knowing what that is.

Direction to Take:
To break out of a rut, try doing the things you do daily in a different way. This could be driving to work with a new route that you haven't used before. Take a class in something you don't think you'd be interested in, and finish it. This can shake things up and get you to quit cycling in an entrenched pattern that is dulling your life.

15 The Devil

16 The Tower

In the beginning, when our lovely solar system was being formed, there were hundreds of protoplanets spinning around and held in thrall by our sun. It was chaos! Planets were shooting around crazily and slamming into each other, and when that happened, the larger ones either absorbed the smaller ones or they broke up and formed moons. This image depicts that happening with our dear Earth and the moon. Maybe the Earth wanted to be a giant water planet, four times her current size? Maybe she had plans for that and that was her dream? Then, out of nowhere, slam! She gets hit by one of the protoplanets, and a piece of her body goes flying out of her, sticks in orbit around her, and becomes the moon. Although she's still mostly water, her dreams of becoming a giant water planet are forever changed.

Divinatory Meaning:
Chaotic change comes out of nowhere.

Direction to Take:
The truth is, it's not what happens to us that affects our lives. It's what we do with it. Sometimes things can happen in life that bring us to our knees, but these moments can create something that is far more brilliant than we could have imagined. Center yourself with the breath when this happens. Just hold space for that. This isn't the time for overthinking. Following the breath allows you to calm yourself and have a degree of inner peace, which creates a strong foundation for great decision making.

16 The Tower

17 The Star

The Star goddess waters the stars that have fallen as freshly made wishes to the garden of Earth. Flowers rise up to greet them.

Divinatory Meaning:
Hopes and dreams are coming true. Hold on to a vision.

Direction to Take:
This is a really good time to invest in a dream. What steps can you take to make it happen for you? Make a treasure map for what you want. Water your dreams. Believe.

17 The Star

18 The Moon

The Moon is an altar for magic, for dreams, for inspiration and hope, where you can place those things that didn't happen and that you want to remember because they helped you become who you are now. It remembers the dreams of the Earth, of the deep mysteries. In this picture, The Moon remembers that the Earth wanted to be a water planet, and it reflects that dream in a sacred pool. Nothing is ever forgotten.

Divinatory Meaning:
Look below the surface. Things are not as they seem. There is a deeper story here.

Direction to Take:
Don't act now. Spend some time looking deeply at things around you. The Moon can talk about either discovering deceptions or uncovering brilliant truths. Meditate on which one that is.

18 The Moon

19 The Sun

An ammonite-horned Earth goddess gazes down at a herd of white horses as they gallop across her body. Blazing like a halo around her lovely head is the solar light of the sun.

Divinatory Meaning:
There is an arrival of happy news in your life. Joyful events. Children bless your life.

Direction to Take:
This card is usually a flying yes for moving forward on something. Also, it's a great time to engage with your inner child. The suggestion is to do things you may have enjoyed as a child: playing jacks, hopscotch, riding a carousel, coloring.

19 The Sun

20 Judgment

This image is of an ancient shaman in a cave placing her handprint on the wall. She is surrounded by crystals. A rainbow of power issues forth from her medicine bowl. She is making time magic here. She is feeling called to unite the deep mystery of the past with the brilliant possibilities of the future. The other handprints are from members of her tribe, and those who have gone before. Whereas Justice is about choosing, Judgment bears the results of that choice. We are the results, the answered prayers, the wishes of ancestors like this.

Divinatory Meaning:
Something is calling you in life; there is a deep, soulful yearning.

Direction to Take:
Your life purpose is revealing itself. How do you want to answer that? Whatever that step is, take it.

20 Judgment

21 The World

In this card, all the four kingdoms come together with the woman who wears a golden gown emblazoned with a DNA double helix. She represents the fifth kingdom of humanity. This card is a hopeful message of all the kingdoms working together in harmony as they all lie languidly around each other, embracing their differences and thereupon finding their similarities. Together we are all The World, for we are all One.

Divinatory Meaning:
Wholeness, completion

Direction to Take:
Finish something you started a long time ago. It will be completed brilliantly if you allow it.

21 The World

Chapter Six
Minor Arcana

The Suite of Kingdoms

A note about the Minor Arcana:

As has been mentioned earlier, there are five suits in this deck. For those of   you
who are familiar with Tarot, and particularly the Rider Waite system, you will observe
some slight differences. In the *Tarot of the Kingdoms*, the Suit of Spirit represents the
querent, the person being read for. In this deck, the Suit of Air represents the East and
equates with wands in the Rider Waite system. The reason for this is that fairies bring
inspiration and are connected to new ideas and creativity, which are qualities of
those who live in the East, and traditionally, that is the direction where fairies live.

Fire is associated with the Kingdom of the South, and dragons and swords have a
long history together. Famous swords have been named after dragons. Swords equate
to action, and so in this deck, the Suit of Fire equates to swords in the Rider Waite system.

From the Kingdom of the West and water hail the merfolk, whose suit equates with
that of cups in the Rider Waite system, for they hold all our dreams and emotions.

The Kingdom of the North, Suit of Earth, equates with pentacles in the Rider Waite
system. The tree beings are even made of earth, and they give knowledge and wisdom
to our physical life, as well as speaking on how we give and receive. This can be seen as
the Suit of Gratitude.

Court cards:

The Page, Knight, Queen, and King of a suit can represent either other people in your life or qualities that you can embrace. Pages are usually representative of apprenticeship situations, messages, and invitations. Knights describe young-adult people in your life or how life is moving for you. Queens represent women in your life, or again, qualities of nurturing leadership you can embrace within yourself. Kings represent men in your life or qualities of action and how you lead with that in your life.

Suit of Spirit
KINGDOM OF THE SELF

THIS card will always represent the one being read for—the querent. Human beings contain all the other kingdoms inside them: air in their lungs, fire in the beat of their heart, earth in their bones, and water in their blood. Yet, there is a fifth element, and that is ether, or spirit. We can move within all these other kingdoms because we contain all of them inside us, and spirit moves inside everything.

There are two ways to use this card. One is to always use it to represent the querent. The second way is to shuffle it with the deck and see where it turns up. In this case, you can then ask the question "Where does the querent's unique light touch this situation?" There can be a sense of presence here. There is something special about them—a gift or talent, a unique point of view—that can especially influence the matter being asked about.

Spirit

Suit of Air
KINGDOM OF THE FAIRIES

WE are the fairies and we love to laugh! You humans are too serious these days. We remember when you used to tell stories around the fire, how you left us presents under trees and at your doorsteps. We like children and animals because they believe. Believing can come first. Do you know how important it is to have an imagination? Imagination is the birth of magic. We're here to help you laugh and play. Also, plant some flowers. We love those.

Ace of Air

A baby fairy nestles inside a dandelion that has gone to seed, ready to be blown out into the world, creating possibilities. Fairies traditionally love the liminal spaces, the in-between times for the day, such as dawn and dusk. Here it is dawn, the birth of a new day.

Divinatory Meaning:
The birth of a new idea. Something wants to be created!

Direction to Take:
Daydream about something you'd like to make happen. Write down what you think. If you write something down, it is ten times more likely to happen.

Two of Air

Two of Air

This is Freya, known by the ancient Norse as the Queen of the Fairies and the original version of the Fairy Godmother. In Norse mythology, Freya wore a cloak made of falcon feathers that allowed her to turn into a falcon. Here she is waving away the pumpkin coach as it races to a certain ball.

Divinatory Meaning:

Successful collaborations. Things are in alignment for success. Making plans.

Direction to Take:

This is you putting your idea out there. Send off those resumes, mail that letter, make those plans, which means leave your house every once in a while. If you want to meet the prince, you have to go to the ball.

Three of Air

A fairy sails on a rainbow bridge in a swan boat. Her arms are uplifted in joy and celebration.

Divinatory Meaning:

Be open to receive the good that is coming to you! The star of success shines over you.

Direction to Take:

Most people think it's polite to decline things like compliments or unexpected gifts. Try saying yes to these things when they appear. Also, this is a great "doing" card for things that need to get done and that excite you.

Four of Air

Four of Air

The fairy wedding. A fairy prince offers a crown to his beloved among spring flowers.

Divinatory Meaning:

Successful partnerships. Traditional card for marriage.

Direction to Take:

Make sure you take time to 'brick in' your successes. This can show up in the form of celebrating your successes, no matter how small. When you celebrate, breathe that in. Sit with it. Fully take it in. This invokes the fairy magic of the four's numerology.

Five of Air

Two fairies refuse to listen to each other as they drift aimlessly in a swamp. Even the bottom feeders swim up to the boat to see what the matter is. A dragonfly tries to shed light on the situation.

Divinatory Meaning:

Conflicts take place that could be resolved by listening or holding space for another person's right to express their view. Competition.

Direction to Take:

This is the drama at the office. You can observe it, but don't get involved. If what you're dealing with is more of a competition, then what can you do differently from what everyone else is doing?

Six of Air

In ancient Greece, it was said that the only people who could ride on the back of the winged horse Pegasus were artists and poets, because Pegasus represented the imagination. He represents inspiration and is bridled and saddled for anyone to ride him who can still dream.

Divinatory Meaning:
Success! Being supported by the enthusiasm and encouragement of your friends and community.

Direction to Take:
While you're experiencing great success in your life, make sure to lift other people up who have supported you. Balance the ego by allowing them to share in your accolade through gratitude.

Seven of Air

A butterfly struggles to get out of its chrysalis. The truth about butterflies is that they are already perfectly formed inside the caterpillar. Once they seal themselves inside the chrysalis, their caterpillar body liquifies and reveals the true form that has always been there within.

Divinatory Meaning:
What you want may require a little more work, but the results are worth it. It may seem like you're up against a lot in life, but you're actually on the threshold of success!

Direction to Take:
You have the upper hand, so the direction is to persevere and dig in.

Eight of Air

Fairies swirl around a tree, causing the flowers to fruit. Dancing like this is how they make magic.

Divinatory Meaning:

Things are about to take off fast! This can indicate travel, possibly to a place where flight is needed to get there.

Direction to Take:

If you receive invitations to travel, accept them, depending on surrounding cards. Also, take time to meditate because it will help you hold your balance when things get really busy.

Nine of Air

In this picture, the fairy maid has made herself as invisible as possible because she doesn't want anyone looking at her, yet she glows brightly because she wants to be seen. The fairy gentleman has heard her call and has come to seek her hand. She really does want him, but there are fears coming up.

Divinatory Meaning:

Readiness. Something new is about to happen in life. It might raise some goose bumps because of its arriving energy. Be brave. You're in a strong position.

Direction to Take:

Remember that nines can deal with illusion. You're stronger than you think you are. There's something coming into your life that you really want but are scared of. Sometimes our minds go toward what could go wrong, but what if it could go right? Step into it.

Ten of Air

Ten of Air

This fairy is a master magician among her kind. Her wings are the colors of the four elements: green for Earth, orange/red for Fire, golden for Air, and blue for Water. She manifests a rainbow, and a kingdom appears on her hand.

Divinatory Meaning:

This is a project brought to fruition. It is the ultimate card in bringing a creative project or idea into physical manifestation.

Direction to Take:

When it comes to your creative dreams, make sure you are carrying only what is for you. Don't bear the burdens of other people's responsibilities.

Page of Air

All pages in Tarot represent invitations or new experiences. This tiny butterfly fairy holds space for a path that lies before you. You can barely see her, and sometimes invitations are like that. They can be subtle in the world of fairy. To find them, you must listen deeply to your personal magic.

Divinatory Meaning:
You will receive an invitation to begin something new and exciting in your life. This will come through a person, the internet, or the mail.

Direction to Take:
What is happening now requires deep listening. That is the direction to take.

Knight of Air

Knight of Air

This fairy is all about dreaming magic. She rides a spirit horse that is perfect for traveling inside the dreamscape. She is accompanied by blue spirit birds that can deliver messages and magic for her. A full moon illuminates their travels.

Divinatory Meaning:

Moving forward in your life. It's okay to take risks. You have support around you.

Direction to Take:

Pay attention to your dreams. If you are moving forward on a new venture, write down the questions you have about it before you go to sleep. Get a magical oil that helps with dreaming. Mugwort is a good one. Smell it before sleep with your questions next to you. You should have some clarity upon waking.

Queen of Air

This fairy queen is riding a pomegranate coach pulled by iridescent peacocks. Traditionally, this card represents a woman who can manifest.

Queen of Air

Divinatory Meaning:

A woman of power who can make things happen for you enters your life. Her appearance can also represent that you have these qualities inside yourself.

Direction to Take:

It's time to step into your manifesting shoes. You have the power to move forward in life. Create that next step.

King of Air

King of Air

This fairy has leprechaun blood in him! He loves music and is dancing on the clouds! If you need his help, he'll step in and help you, but he'll wait till the last minute to do so. Why? Because he doesn't want to rob you of the experience of knowing you're capable and strong.

Divinatory Meaning:
An exciting man who appreciates you enters your life. He won't do everything for you, though. Creative leadership skills.

Direction to Take:
Be assertive with what you want. It's somebody else's job to tell you no, and the answer will always be no unless you ask.

Suit of Fire
KINGDOM OF THE DRAGONS

WE dragons have always been a part of Earth's history. We work closely with the angels and the phoenixes. We are eternal beings, so we don't have the same concept of time you have. For us, everything is in a state of becoming. If you look at a rose bud and then compare it to a fully bloomed rose, you can see where the bud will become the rose. You know it will not become a sunflower. This is a basic lesson in alchemy. Think of who you want to be, in the highest state of yourself as a being. How are you in your state of becoming?

Ace of Fire

The phoenix rises from the ashes of an old dream it had.

Divinatory Meaning:
A birth of something new. Sometimes a troubling birth, but it rises brilliantly.

Direction to Take:
Here there is an action on your part that is required. Take that step.

Two of Fire

These two dragons are from different realms in the dragon world. How will they come together in relationship? One is an Earth dragon, the other one Fire. Two opposing forces that form a heart are shown here.

Two of Fire

Divinatory Meaning:
What one lacks, the other can give. If in a stuck situation, find the value in what the other has to offer.

Direction to Take:
This indicates that there is no action to take at this time. This card can talk about trusting in the Divine unfoldment in the universe. When you surrender in this way, the Divine can step in and do the heavy lifting.

Three of Fire

Three of Fire

There is an old Druidic legend that states that the dragons left the physical world so humans could experience the Age of Reason. When they departed, they left trails that formed lines of power all over the Earth, called ley lines. This is a picture of a dragon slipping into the Earth and leaving a ley line in his wake.

Divinatory Meaning:
The end of a relationship or situation in your life

Direction to Take:
Find the courage in you to bring something to an end that is no longer serving you.

Four of Fire

This dragon is a bud dragon. She likes to nestle like a bulb deep in the earth, where plants grow. She glows and vibrates like a heart from a rose. Her loving energy feeds the plants above her.

Divinatory Meaning:
Be in a space of holding. What that means is you need to rest and hold your dreams to you, feeding them quietly. Hold space for yourself. Rome wasn't built in a day.

Direction to Take:
This calls for meditation. Sometimes with this card, there is something more that hasn't revealed itself yet. Patience.

Five of Fire

Five of Fire

We encounter our first angel, an angel of Divine Light. This angel wants to express the idea of the Fire Kingdom in its purest form. Coming from a high place, he says there is always a right action to take that harms none and blesses all. That is the action to take.

Divinatory Meaning:
An opportunity to do the right thing

Direction to Take:
Although this may require tremendous courage on your part, this is about speaking your truth and acting from that place, even if your voice shakes.

Six of Fire

Two dragon beings ride in a flying ship. You can see they have wings themselves, but it's nice to get a little help from the Universe. The lady dragon is enjoying the journey, dropping flaming flowers into the sky, while the dragon fellow, with a little concern, is wondering where they are going.

Divinatory Meaning:

This card is about trust. Sixes can speak of assistance that comes to you. You're not going to be doing all the work yourself. There are parts of the upcoming path for you that are unknown, and that is okay. Trust in the direction you are heading in. Life is getting better; you just can't see it yet.

Direction to Take:

Have an awareness that things aren't always as they appear. There is a new direction emerging in your life. Relax.

Seven of Fire

Seven of Fire

A dragon man has fallen asleep right before the finish line. He is the source of his own treasure yet isn't aware of it as he sleeps on it. Before him is that glittering kingdom where all his dreams would come true.

Divinatory Meaning:

Be alert. Something powerful is coming to you, and you have to be awake to grasp it.

Direction to Take:

Pay attention. The next step is to take some time and carefully study what is around you.

Eight of Fire

This lovely dragon lady is distracted by the butterflies yet is held by the hand by an angel. Whenever we're distracted and there are things we need to get done, know that our guides always have us by the hand.

Divinatory Meaning:

Usually when this card turns up, there are minor dramas going on in life. Sometimes you can feel trapped by them.

Direction to Take:

Don't sweat the small stuff.

Nine of Fire

Nine of Fire

This beautiful Asian dragon says that where she lives, dragons don't have wings. They don't need them. The way their bodies are designed, they just float like a ribbon caught in the wind, gently gliding and being guided by the air currents. She said it has a great deal to do with trust—knowing that her body will just launch gracefully into the sky and be suspended by invisible forces. It's like dancing.

Divinatory Meaning:
Needless worry. Being stuck in your head. The things that are being worried about have not manifested on the physical plane.

Direction to Take:
Release fear. Relax. Don't borrow trouble about tomorrow.

Ten of Fire

The three dragons represent dawn, noon, and midnight. They are a gateway to a new adventure.

Ten of Fire

Divinatory Meaning:

The Kingdom of the South is all about the perfect action steps to take next. Think of these three dragons as allies that help you embark on your next journey in life. A long time ago, they say, you asked for a new lease on life, and here it is. But you have to pay for that kind of magic by leaving behind what has been known before. Closure.

Direction to Take:

You need to close the door on something that isn't working for you, whether that is a relationship or a job, or something else. Move on.

Page of Fire

Page of Fire

This Page of Fire is mischievous! He is a lot of fun and can perform all kinds of interesting magic! Sometimes he comes into your life to trick you into doing good if you aren't paying attention.

Divinatory Meaning:
A service done for or against you in secret

Direction to Take:
Pay attention to who your allies are in your life. This can also indicate that it's time to consider your options from a new perspective.

Knight of Fire

A lady rides on the back of her secret lover, a powerful dragon. A full harvest moon illuminates them like a halo.

Knight of Fire

Divinatory Meaning:

Swift new developments in life. A romantic interest sweeping you off your feet.

Direction to Take:

Find a way to balance yourself so that when things take off, you're not overwhelmed by what or who is coming in and how fast things are moving.

Queen of Fire

The Queen of Fire, of the Dragons, knows her own worth. Magic springs forth from her just by living and breathing, and she leaves it like stardust wherever she goes. She is comfortable in her own skin. Can represent a powerful woman who shoots straight from the hip.

Divinatory Meaning:

A strong, powerful woman enters your life. She knows who she is and cuts to the chase when she speaks. She wants you to know it's okay to be yourself. You don't have to dress up for company.

Direction to Take:

Be open to the advice of a strong woman who will tell it like it is. If this represents you, then you need to be more clear about what you want.

King of Fire

The King of Fire merges the draconic, angelic, and phoenix world into his being. A master of the element of Fire, he is also nurturing because Fire is the element that rules the heart in Chinese medicine. It can be both destructive, as in a forest fire, or nurturing, like the fire burning in a hearth.

Divinatory Meaning:

There is a passionate, powerful, and brutally honest man who is interested in helping you in some way. A great business partner or backer.

Direction to Take:

Embody the energy of what the King of the Dragons would feel like to you, and let that guide your next steps with compassion and grace.

Suit of Water
KINGDOM OF THE MERMAIDS

WE, the Merkingdom, welcome you to the place where all dreaming happens. Water has a magnetic quality to it, magically speaking, and we are always collecting your feelings and memories that you leave in the water when you play in it. Did you know that there are both freshwater and saltwater mermaids? The freshwater ones tend to isolate and are more introverted, whereas the saltwater mermaids live in cities under the sea. We have both come together to offer you our wisdom. Welcome!

Ace of Water

This mermom-to-be says you can't see her baby yet, but you can see the happiness and joy around it. She invites you to feel joyful right now. Lotuses bloom in the waters around her.

Divinatory Meaning:
New birth. The beginning of happiness and joy.

Direction to Take:
Open your heart. Let love in.

Two of Water

This mermaid said she fell in love with a sailor. She heard him on his ship make a wish for a different kind of love, and she showed up. She was very different from what he was expecting, but he was intrigued, and so they started seeing each other.

Divinatory Meaning:
Meeting someone new. New partnerships.

Direction to Take:
Be open to new people coming into your life.

Three of Water

This is the traditional card in the Tarot of falling in love. These merfolk are intertwined and oblivious to all else around them. The ocean formed this pink halo of light around them.

Divinatory Meaning:

Celebration. True love.

Direction to Take:

It's time to get out there in the world and meet people. Accept social invitations that seem interesting to you.

Four of Water

This mermaid is modeling boredom. She says it can happen. Out in the ocean or on some of the lakes the freshwater mermaids live in, the skies get gray and the waves are choppy or monotonous. Here she is, sitting on an outcropping of rock while hidden treasure shimmers beneath her.

Divinatory Meaning:

An offer comes from left field. Boredom or being jaded, yet those two feelings are opportunities for something wonderful and completely different to come into your life!

Direction to Take:

Pay attention to exciting offers that come from completely different directions. You will not expect this.

Five of Water

This mermaid is turning to shell. She's so deep in her reminiscing about life, nursing old memories, that she completely lives in the past, and her lovely tail is turning to shell. She won't be able to swim that way. She can unkink herself, of course, but it will take some stretching.

Divinatory Meaning:
Don't get caught up in the could've, should've, would've. Life is always bringing new, fresh experiences.

Direction to Take:
Focus on the present moment and the blessings you have now. When you demonstrate that kind of gratitude, more doors open to you than you can ever dream of.

Six of Water

These merchildren have hidden their favorite things on the ocean bottom so they can find them later when they grow up. They call them "half-remembered treasures," because when they find them again, they "half remember" why they hid them in the first place when they were little, and they get to reinvent their specialness by building new memories around them. This is a lot of fun!

Divinatory Meaning:

People you haven't seen in a long time will turn up in your life. Also, old treasures return to you. Inheritance.

Direction to Take:

There is energy around a childhood dream you once had. There is something that wants to be expressed from it. Connect with what that is.

Seven of Water

This is a card of a mermaid who has it all. That's the thing with having your dreams come true. Sometimes when they do, they don't quite feel like what you thought they would. She sits atop a large outcropping of rock while lotuses the color of the chakras bloom around her, each holding a different dream.

Divinatory Meaning:

A lot of opportunities lie before you. Which one will you choose?

Direction to Take:

Daydream about possibilities.

Eight of Water

A mermaid reaches for a world that is completely foreign to her natal element. It is just beyond her. Can she have it? And if so, what must she do to get there?

Divinatory Meaning:

Reaching for something that is close enough, yet far away. Wanting something that may not bring you the happiness you think it will. What do you really wish for?

Direction to Take:

Be sure that what you're reaching for is worth it. Sometimes to get what you want out of life, it's more expedient to align with how you want to feel after you've attained it, rather than the particular goal itself. When you focus on the feeling state you want to feel, you can create an openness in your life where the Universe can show you how brilliantly creative it can be with fulfilling that desire you have.

Nine of Water

The Nine of Water is the traditional wish card in the Tarot, and whenever it shows up in a reading it means you can make a wish. A mermother reaches for her baby. She has many things in life that bring her great happiness, and the baby is one of them. A rainbow shines down on their happiness.

Divinatory Meaning:
A wish fulfilled

Direction to Take:
Seriously. Make a wish.

Ten of Water

A merfamily holds on to one another on a starry night. Stars illuminate the night sky. Love is all around them.

Divinatory Meaning:
Having it all emotionally. A happy celebration with others. Finding your soul family. Feeling like you belong.

Direction to Take:
You have a right to be happy. Find your happy place.

Page of Water

These merchildren have found a message in a bottle! What's inside? The sky is stormy around them, and they seem very interested in the story before them.

Divinatory Meaning:
Invitations to social events. New relationship possibilities.

Direction to Take:
Learn something new that is creative. Be open to the possibility of new love.

Knight of Water

This knight is very creative. He is holding a lotus chalice full of a liquid that will bring you what you most need in life. He's also a hopeless romantic as he rides his gallant seahorse.

Divinatory Meaning:

Life may start flowing more sweetly for you now. A new romantic interest, but one that may not last—more like a summer romance.

Direction to Take:

This is an invitation to become more fluid in life. Express your inner poet. Go out on dates that intrigue you.

Queen of Water

This merqueen has a radiant heart. She sits on her shell throne encrusted with crystals.

Divinatory Meaning:

Listen to your dreams and feel into the heart space with them. Indicates a loving, nurturing woman in your life or coming into those qualities yourself.

Direction to Take:

Get in touch with your emotions. They can be an excellent guidance system for you right now.

King of Water

The King of the West holds his baby in his arms. Even though the ocean is wild, he is perfectly balanced and calm as he shows her the world.

Divinatory Meaning:

The Kingdom of the West says you have a nurturing influence in your life; although it may not always be there, it will lift you up when you most need it so that you can see other options available to you. A nurturing and caring male influence is in your life or will soon appear.

Direction to Take:

Lead from the heart. Get centered in that space and ask the question "What would love do?" Then be receptive to the answer.

Suit of Earth
KINGDOM OF THE TREE BEINGS

WE are the tree spirits. We know how to give and receive in such perfection that we don't feel the need to get up and go after it. That is why we are rooted on the spot. We are excellent at holding space for a long time. We know what it is to be in gratitude. We even feel that this could be called the suit of gratefulness, of a full heart. No matter what happens in life, the Earth is always singing, "I love you, I love you, I love you." Can you hear the music?

115

Ace of Earth

A tree made of foliate hands holds a baby in a loving embrace.

Divinatory Meaning:
Feeling connected for the first time to something beautiful in life. New birth. New abundance and sources of income.

Direction to Take:
Look for new opportunities in your life to enhance things in your physical world. This can be a new job, a new opportunity to improve health, or a relationship. This is something new, not anything you've done before.

Two of Earth

Have you ever been out in nature and seen trees grow right out of cliffsides? It seems impossible that they could grow in such a compromising place, yet they do.

Divinatory Meaning:

You may feel like you're juggling things right now; even so, you are completely supported by the divine Universe. When you surrender to the place you are in right now, the Divine can step in and do the heavy lifting. Then grace can flow through your life.

Direction to Take:

There is a secondary source of support near you. Where is it? Sometimes this can manifest as something else that can help, like a second job, a supportive friend, or even an animal that loves you.

Three of Earth

Three of Earth

These tree spirits are locked in an embrace of purest love and are intertwined around each other in a kiss. Even the sun blesses them, forming a halo around them.

Divinatory Meaning:

Flourishing of a relationship. Mastering the art of gratitude. A blessing coming your way.

Direction to Take:

Talk to everybody you meet. As if they matter. You never know who can be a source of something good in your life. This isn't why you talk to them, but when you build this kind of connectedness, you'll be like the trees, who connect to each other through their roots, building vast webs of support and love.

Four of Earth

It's winter, and this tree spirit is holding herself while deep in meditation. There is a lot happening here, although it looks like nothing is happening. During winter, it's very busy under the ground, with everyone getting ready for spring. The snow falls gently around her.

Four of Earth

Divinatory Meaning:
Now is a time to focus and to gather your resources. Investing.

Direction to Take:
Take care of yourself. Take a nap. Don't overspend. Be conservative with your finances.

Five of Earth

This mother tree is sheltering a flower. Behind her is a ring of trees in the distance. They seem so far away, but they encircle her and she protects the flower.

Divinatory Meaning:

This card can indicate how isolating it can feel when things aren't going well with either finances or health. We can feel despair, forgetting that we were always supported by the Divine Universe.

Direction to Take:

When times are down, look for support. It's out there. It also indicates that the best step to take is some self-care. This card usually indicates a source of help that is available to you that you aren't seeing. It's there. Right in front of you. Look at it.

Six of Earth

The tree spirit in this card is embodying generosity by showering gifts upon the Earth from the back of a foliate stag.

Divinatory Meaning:

Receiving a windfall. Also, this card says you can be a blessing to another by what you can give.

Direction to Take:

Be open to receiving. Also, understand that even if you don't have any money, you always have something to give, whether it's time, a good listening ear, or something else.

Seven of Earth

Seven of Earth

Four trees in various seasons grace a crossroads. Clockwise from the top, they are winter, summer, spring, and fall.

Divinatory Meaning:

Crossroads of life. You've worked hard to get where you're at. Do you want to continue going for it or change and do something else?

Direction to Take:

Look at the card. Which tree are you drawn to? It it's the top tree, then you are entering winter in your life, and the advice is to stay where you are and take no action. If it's the fruiting tree to the right, then it's time to continue working on what you want and to move forward. If it's the bottom tree, which is just entering spring, then you must nurture and support something so that it can be given birth to. If you're drawn to the tree on the left, then fall is coming, so it's a time to finish up loose ends and enjoy life at some fall parties.

Eight of Earth

This tree spirit is dancing in her own way, with the aurora borealis as a veil.

Eight of Earth

Divinatory Meaning:
More than one way to express a talent that you have. Working on a creative project that will bear fruit. Learning something new.

Direction to Take:
There is more to learn about what you are engaged in. Take more training or a class. This can be one of the going-back-to-school cards.

Nine of Earth

This tree is a giving tree, a tree of the winter season. She shelters love and compassion, two sprites that bless the season of fullness in your life.

Divinatory Meaning:

Everything comes together for you. Crowned with success.

Direction to Take:

Enjoy the fruits of your labor. Can also indicate a good time to invest or buy.

Ten of Earth

In the Ten of Earth, the tree goddess is connected fully with all that is good and beautiful in the Universe. She knows where she comes from, and her ancestry sings through her roots. She offers their gifts through her branches, once those gifts mix with her personal alchemy.

Divinatory Meaning:

Connecting on a deep level with your ancestral line. An opportunity to be blessed by family. Inheritance.

Direction to Take:

Connect with your community or family. Gather with them, whether it's to enjoy their company or to build something.

Ten of Earth

Page of Earth

Page of Earth

In the distant past, wolves would den in the middle of sown fields, and when they emerged to go hunting, they would oftentimes be covered in the leaves of whatever had been planted. The ancient Celts believed they were foliate beings like the Green Man, and when they saw a wolf come out of the fields, they said it was "the wolf of the woods." This one howls into the night, and the aurora borealis spills out of its singing.

Divinatory Meaning:
You have been invited to share your gifts with the world. You have a place in this world, and you must claim it. An event or significant meeting may happen where you feel aligned with your true purpose.

Direction to Take:
Pay attention for invitations approaching. They are doors to new opportunities.

Knight of Earth

This is the Green Man, a foliate being who bears a cornucopia. He rides a foliate Clydesdale. These horses are known for pulling massive loads and, concerning abundance, can speak of great financial opportunities coming your way, although it may take its time getting there.

Divinatory Meaning:
Success is coming to you, although it may arrive later in the week, the month, or the season. Once it arrives, it will have longevity and abide with you for a long time.

Direction to Take:
Exercise patience. Stick to it.

Queen of Earth

This earth mother glimmers with crystals as she grows new life inside her. With one hand she embraces her child, while she holds the world in her other hand. She has so much love to give.

Divinatory Meaning:
A nurturing woman with resources comes into your life. She is not only full of resources, but resourceful as well.

Direction to Take:
Stop worrying about your health or your money.

King of Earth

This great stag is the Forest Spirit, the King of Earth. He is made from earth and can spring up anywhere. He protects all things wild. Within his antlers, he holds the universe.

King of Earth

Divinatory Meaning:
A strong, successful, nurturing man comes into your life. He is resourceful and full of magic. You have these qualities yourself.

Direction to Take:
Consult a friend who is mastering life the way you want to.

Chapter Seven
Extra Card

A NOTE FROM THE UNIVERSE

HERE you are, sitting in your lotus having tea. The lotus floats in that liminal part of the physical universe where nothing is created yet, but wants to be. Things look a little strange here, as the space that is the starry orb of the sky looks almost like water that your lovely lotus is floating on.

Rising from the amniotic waters of this part of the universe, we witness the idea of a planet being born—not the physical planet itself, but the idea of it. For you see, you are in the Place Where the Souls of Planets Are Born. An umbilical cord that connects the new planet soul to the heart of the universe contains a moon in it, so this planet will have one.

The physical universe wanted you to know this:

That sometimes you will come into this world as a human being, but that if you want to at some point during your journey of incarnation, you can be born as a planet. It's a big deal to be the soul of a planet. You have to have that life for billions of years, and other life forms may live on you.

You can create worlds here as a human being, or you can be a world that creates beings out in the physical universe.

The Universe

You don't have to do it if you don't want to. The physical universe just wanted you to know that that's how life happens for planets and stars too—first it's a soul that is created. Then it finds a form.

Divinatory Meaning:

Seeing things from a deeper, bigger perspective

Direction to Take:

To get yourself out of thinking or acting small, ask the question "Who is observing here?"

Chapter Eight
Finding Your Purpose

MOST people, when they come in for a reading and want to know what their purpose is, often confuse "purpose" with a job or career. In this chapter, we will address finding one's purpose, which goes far deeper than career or job, into the essence of who you are here to be. From that place, job and career choices can be sought after, but these do not define you. I find that most people overly identify how they perceive one another through what they do for a living. Everyone has to pay the bills. A different way of looking at life is that your job doesn't define you; your hobbies do. The fact that you cultivate orchids or write poetry says more about you as a person than what you do to bring down a paycheck. Everybody has some work they do to take care of the basic needs of life, and whatever that is can have little to do with who you are, yet we often use it as a ruler to measure each other with.

The technique that we will be discussing can reveal not just your life's purpose but can also be used to look into the purpose or main focus for the month, the year, or even a specific goal you have. For this type of reading, we will be separating the Major Arcana out from the deck and using only the 22 trumps.

Think of your purpose. What do you want to know about it? Do you

- want to know what it is?
- want to know what the higher purpose is for the year? Or the month?
- want to know the purpose for a specific goal? In this case, you are exploring the deeper theme that may be sitting quietly behind a goal you want for reason "x," but the Divine is moving you to do for reason "y." This type of reading will reveal the "y."

Write down your question, because you may want to reflect or journal about it after. Shuffle the 22 cards. Then cut them face down so they form three piles from right to left. Then pick up the piles from right to left with your left hand, because that hand goes straight to the heart.

Flip the deck over so you can see the images on the cards. While still holding the entire deck in your hand, look for the Judgment card. Once you find it, pull it out, plus the card that comes before it and the card that comes after it.

Judgment is the card that talks about a Higher Purpose, because it is the card where you are traditionally called to something greater than yourself. In the Rider Waite deck, this card depicts Archangel Gabriel blowing the horn at Judgment Day to call everyone home, and you can see people rising out of their graves to answer that call.

So here, we are using Judgment to represent the concept of the Higher Purpose. The card that comes before it represents the influence that has brought you to this place of discovery. The card that comes after it indicates the goal, or where you are headed.

How these are read is not the same as how you would read them in a typical reading. As opposed to looking at a predictive element, what we are interested in is the essence of what the card means. For example, let's say you pull the Moon, Judgment, and the World.

What led you to where you are is the deep mystery, wanting to know more about the secret, inner workings of creation. This is evidenced by the Moon; this is the Moon's essence. We don't "read" Judgment, the next card, because it is simply representing the concept of Higher Purpose and holding space for that.

The next card placed after Judgment is the World. Reflecting on the deep mystery, this person has a purpose of sharing what they've learned with the world and making it accessible to everyone. In this case, the World represents what can be physically known. This particular Higher Purpose reading was done for a shaman, interestingly enough.

I have provided a list of possible interpretations, but please do not limit what you find to what is here when you do this spread. Tap into your intuition. See this three-card Higher Purpose spread as a trilogy of movies you're going to see, utilizing the technique from chapter one.

THE CARD BEFORE

THE FOOL If this card comes before, you may be feeling lost and unsure. Nothing is particularly calling you—or everything is.

THE MAGICIAN The essence is about a strong desire to make something or create something that will be remembered. You want to be remembered.

THE HIGH PRIESTESS A strong desire to explore the unknown

THE EMPRESS A longing to create. You may not perceive yourself as even having a skill set for making things or nurturing things, so this can be a calling to discover that you have talents the world needs.

THE EMPEROR The essence is the desire to protect something.

THE HIEROPHANT Wanting to make a difference in the world

THE LOVERS This is connected to two different concepts: wanting to do the right thing and/or wanting life to be more romantic or interesting in some way.

THE CHARIOT	A strong desire to rise above your circumstances
STRENGTH	How to get something done when you're dealing with difficult personalities or work situations. Also may address wanting to improve health.
THE HERMIT	A strong desire to know yourself outside of other people
THE WHEEL OF FORTUNE	A desire for magic and learning techniques of manifestation. A desire to influence or be an influencer.
JUSTICE	Feeling called to pursue a path that not everyone will agree with or support you on
THE HANGED MAN	Struggling with giving something up that you've outgrown
DEATH	Feeling the urge for a change that frightens you but is one you dream of on the deepest levels of self
TEMPERANCE	Stepping into the shoes of a muse. Great creativity is here.
THE DEVIL	Wanting to solve something that is disturbing you

THE TOWER	An urge to be a mover and shaker

THE STAR	Having a dream that is important to you. Can indicate that what drives you is a childhood dream; even if it seems fanciful or unattainable, the idea of it inspires you deeply.

THE MOON	The urge to uncover mysteries, search for new discoveries, becoming an adept.

THE SUN	Play and seeing life as enjoyable and positive is a strong motivator.

THE WORLD	What you are currently observing in the physical world, other countries, or other cultures is a strong motivator for you.

WHERE IT IS LEADING

THE FOOL	The goal is to bring fresh approaches to life. Here there is inventiveness and doing something differently than others have seen before.

THE MAGICIAN The goal is to create something physical in the world that others can marvel at.

THE HIGH PRIESTESS The goal is to become a keeper of secrets. Doing services for others in secret, collecting the mystery. Writing mysteries, uncovering mysteries.

THE EMPRESS Building something physical that others enjoy. Something that nurtures and cares for living things, whether it's people, children, animals, or plants.

THE EMPEROR There is a goal of protecting and building something that has boundaries so that those within can be safe.

THE HIEROPHANT Becoming a leader. Teaching others is here, even if it is not your profession. There is a hint of the powers of the Fairy Godmother here, where you have the power to help or bless others.

THE LOVERS Having a romantic life. This can either be with another person, so then the goal is to allow yourself to be loved, or, it's having a romantic life: drink the good wine, always have flowers on your dinner table, read poetry or write poetry, etc.

THE CHARIOT This indicates a need for travel and that your purpose is fulfilled through travel, a global presence, online stuff, or meeting people from other places.

STRENGTH — Doing physical things like hiking, running marathons, or assisting others in those things. Floral essences and herbalism show up here too.

THE HERMIT — Having a deep, spiritual practice that resonates with you. From this place of purpose, you are aligned with your inner bell, and great things can come from this place, although they may be veiled in simplicity.

THE WHEEL OF FORTUNE — Divination is here. Also, your purpose is aligned with bringing change to the world.

JUSTICE — The goal is about how to make the best decisions. This can be connected with helping others with what is right and fair. This can indicate a strong sense of destiny.

THE HANGED MAN — This can be one of the most profound purposes of all, because it involves completely surrendering to what is. It can indicate a strong spiritual calling. It can also indicate a desire to trust completely in what the Divine has in store for you. Here, life can be an adventure.

DEATH Breaking up old things to bring in new things. Working with death or sleep magic, which is how to cultivate your skills being a lucid dreamer.

TEMPERANCE This card wants to cook for other people, or bake. Make wine. Do things that make people comfortable around each other or enjoy the company of each other. Exploring healing modalities is here.

THE DEVIL When The Devil is the goal, it is a calling that maybe you're just here to enjoy life. Life wants to express itself more sensually to you. Take up belly dancing or salsa dancing. Enjoy the taste of food. It's about digging into this physical existence with gusto.

THE TOWER Here is where the greatest alchemy can happen. You have a skill set to turn straw into gold. You can help others rise from disaster to claim a better destiny. A lot of great art is created from deconstructing something. You can see possibilities where no one else can.

THE STAR Astrology likes to be here. Beyond that, this is about always being in alignment with your North Star. It's absolute trust in your intuition. It can also involve things dealing with the stars and space, and navigating by that.

THE MOON This is the card for the explorer. The essence is about doing the archeology of what lies hidden below the surface. A quest to explore and uncover.

| THE SUN | Helping children or young people. Bringing light to dark places. |
| THE WORLD | Connecting with the people of the world, or the world in general. This is a global reach, although it can also represent a strong desire to build or connect with a specific community. |

Approach exploring your Higher Purpose with a lightness of touch. Engage playfulness when you do this, because you'll become more open to receiving good messages when you're relaxed. Another way you can divine the meanings of the cards in this spread is to step into each card that is being read. For that, all you do is imagine that the border of the card in question is a door frame. Imagine that the card is life size, and visualize yourself stepping through that door frame.

From there, explore the images in the card. If there are living beings depicted in the card, whether human or animal, have a conversation with them. What do they have to tell you? Talk to the colors in the card. Maybe there are different things you'll discover in the card behind the door frame than aren't pictured in the card. What are they? Journal about these things.

If you do this before bed, you may get some interesting dreams that may enlighten you further. Note those down. Become an archeologist of your own psyche.

Chapter Nine
Tarot Alchemy

THE ANCIENT art of alchemy centered itself around the belief that one could make gold out of combining base elements like lead, for example, with a mysterious ingredient called "the Philosopher's Stone." Some have disputed that the true purpose of the alchemists wasn't to make gold, but to purify the spirit to its highest level from its baser qualities. The Philosopher's Stone, in that case, was the process by which one accomplished this, whether that mysterious ingredient was a meditation or a magical process. Either way, the goal was transformation, whether we are talking about making gold or transforming the spirit.

There are many stories about alchemy in the world of fairy tales, where a young maid with the help of an imp named Rumpelstiltskin turns straw into gold. Through the journey of the Major Arcana, we can see transformation and alchemy happening with each of the cards. In this chapter, we are going to speak of how to practice a certain kind of alchemy—the art of turning something base, or unsatisfactory—to the gold of manifestation. I learned this technique when I was studying runes many years ago and have found that it works brilliantly with Tarot.

What I learned was that what most people who divine the future, past, and present don't know is that while you are in the space of a reading, the Door to Fate is open. Once

you begin a reading, you have opened the   door, and
until the reading is completed, you are in that hallowed space
of possibility. You can transform negative circumstances here and do a little
magic. I like to call the method I will share with you here Tarot Alchemy.

This is how it happens. When you're doing a reading and a lot of cards
indicating negativity turn up in the reading, you can invite the querent to change
things if they wish. How you do this is that you select no more than three cards that foretell
negative energies, whether they have occurred in the past, present, or future positions of
the spread you're working with. You start with the first card and have the querent pick it
up with their dominant hand, saying, "I now remove this card and all that it means from
the Law of Cause and Effect." Place this card to the side.

Shuffle the rest of the deck that has not been used for the spread you have laid down.
Ask the cards for an answer, a transformative energy to help the reading transcend to a
more helpful place. You can say to yourself as you shuffle, "Straw to gold, straw to gold,
straw to gold." Hand the deck to the querent and have them select a card at random. The
card selected will be a card of alchemy. With their receptive hand (the hand they don't
write with), have them place the new card in the place that they pulled the old card out
of, saying, "I now bring in my highest and best good."

Do the same if there are other cards that you are pulling. I've found that this completely
shifts their fortunes for them, and helps them feel empowered.

The card that is selected, if it is a "negative" card, can shed light on why these
things have occurred and what to do to change it. If it is a more "positively" aspected

card, then there is a lot of good energy around the querent that is made available to them through their guides, particularly their guardian angel. I've seen this kind of alchemy even change the energy of things in the past! In some cases, it has even changed how people in their lives remembered things. This is deep magic, and you have to really feel it to offer this kind of alchemy for yourself or someone else.

It is powerful when it happens because you can engage directly with the Akashic Records, a cosmic library where your Life Plan is kept. You have your own book there. You can change things from this place during a reading.

Our lives are lived out in alchemy. We are always given opportunities to either stay with something or someone or to change it. When we move forward to bring change in our lives, we are stepping into the shoes of the alchemist. We all have these powers to do so.

This deck is a way to work with the power of the Sacred Directions and the magical beings that hail from those kingdoms that lie within them. You are never alone in your journey of life, unless you wish to be. The light to illuminate your path is always available to you when you ask for it, and these merry denizens of the other kingdoms will happily walk that path with you.

Blessed be.